SPA 102

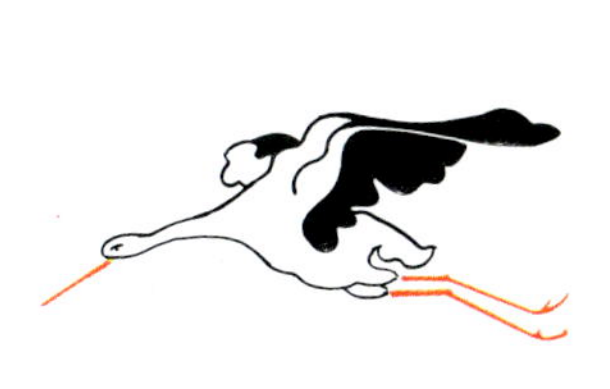

SPA 103

SPA 124
Escadrille Lafayette

SPA 124

SPA 150

SPA 151

SPA 152

SPA 153

SPA 155

SPA 156

SPA 158

SPA 159

SPA 160

SPA 161

SPA 162

SPA 166

SPA 172

SPA 314

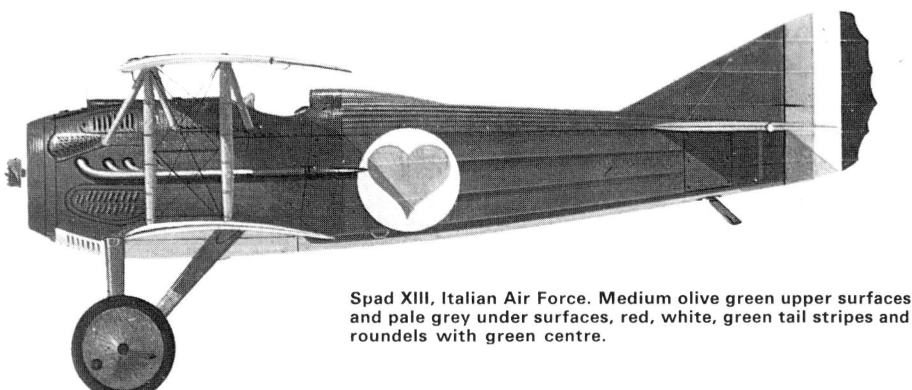

Spad XIII, Italian Air Force. Medium olive green upper surfaces and pale grey under surfaces, red, white, green tail stripes and roundels with green centre.

SPAD SCOUTS SVII-SXIII

**Illustrated by
Michael P. Roffe
and Richard Ward**

**Text and Compiled by
J. M. Bruce**

ACKNOWLEDGEMENTS

Grateful thanks are extended to all who assisted with photographs and information making possible the publication of this pictorial survey of the Spad Scouts S.VII and S.XIII. Thanks to all those who assisted whose names are listed below in alphabetical order.

Warren M. Bodie, Peter M. Bowers, J. B. Cynk, Fred C. Dickey Jr., Peter M. Grosz, Egon Krueger, P. R. Little, Jean Noël, Zdeněk Titz, Imperial War Museum, Royal Aeronautical Society, Ministry of Defence, Flight International, Musée Royal de l'Armée et d'Histoire Militaire Brussels, E. C. Armée.

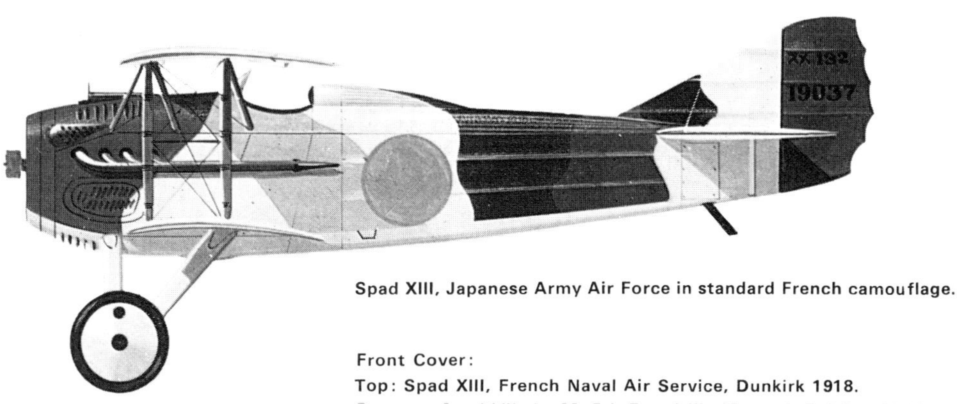

Spad XIII, Japanese Army Air Force in standard French camouflage.

Front Cover:
Top: Spad XIII, French Naval Air Service, Dunkirk 1918.
Bottom: Spad VII, Sp.22, 5th Escadrille 'Comet', Belgian Air Force.

PUBLISHED BY

Arco Publishing Company, Inc., 219 Park Avenue South, New York, N.Y. 10003

First Published by Osprey Publications Ltd. and Printed in Great Britain

Library of Congress No. 77-93931 · Library Edition SBN 668-02112-8 · Paperback Edition SBN 668-02110-1

Spad VII S.116 flown by Adjudant Maxime Lenoir in Esc. SPA 23 in 1916. The personal marking, "Le" and a negro's head, is a rebus on Lenoir's name.   (Photo: Jean Noël)

S.3281, a Spad VII of Esc. SPA 99.

SPAD SCOUTS SVII - SXIII

One of the supreme aerial weapons of the first world war was the French Spad single-seat fighter in its various forms. Its success was the more remarkable in view of its descent from a series of undistinguished (and in some cases outlandish) predecessors that had emerged from the works of the *Société anonyme pour l'Aviation et ses Dérivés*. These included the freakish Spad A.2 and A.4 in which the gunner's cockpit was mounted in front of the aircraft's tractor airscrew.

In April 1916 the Spad Type V appeared. This was a clean, compact single-seater, wholly conventional in appearance, yet embodying several structural features that had appeared in the Spad A.2 and A.4. The most notable of these were the unusual interplane bracing and the method of actuating the ailerons, which were fitted to the upper wings only. Careful attention to structural design gave the Type V an airframe of immense strength.

Louis Béchereau, the chief designer of the S.P.A.D., had been fortunate in being able to design the new Spad type round the excellent new 140-h.p. Hispano-Suiza 8A engine designed by Marc Birkigt. Also in early prospect was a gun-synchronizing mechanism designed for this engine by Birkigt.

The Spad Type V made its first flight in the hands of the company's test pilot, Béquet, and is said to have attained a speed of 215 km/hr (134 m.p.h.) on that occasion. Such a speed seems unlikely, but the aircraft's performance was undoubtedly very good and greatly impressed the French authorities when it underwent official trials at Villacoublay in May 1916. The Spad's performance was substantially better than that of the Nieuport scouts then in general use in the *escadrilles de chasse* of the *Aviation militaire*, and an initial order for 268 production aircraft was placed forthwith.

The first contract was awarded to the parent firm, who started production in the summer of 1916. The aircraft delivered to the *Aviation militaire* were designated Spad VII and were powered by the Hispano-Suiza 8Aa engine, which delivered 150 h.p. at 1,450 r.p.m. and 175 h.p. at 1,700 r.p.m. (It should be noted that many

French Spads VII bore the marking "140 hp Hispano-Suiza" on the rudder when fitted with the 8Aa engine, which was more usually referred to as the 150-h.p. Hispano-Suiza.) Armament was a single 7.65 mm. Vickers machine-gun with Birkigt synchronizing gear, mounted slightly to starboard of centre. The ammunition was carried in continuous canvas belts wound on to large-diameter drums.

Long exhaust pipes terminating just abaft the cockpit ran along the fuselage sides; that on the port side served as a step. The main fuel tank was mounted under the lower wing and was shaped to conform to the contours of the belly fairing of the fuselage. It had a device for jettisoning its contents in emergency, and the Spad VII must have been the first operational aircraft to have this safety device.

One early Spad VII had a 150-h.p. Renault engine. Like the Hispano-Suiza, the Renault was a water-cooled V-8, but its exhaust valves were on the inboard sides of its cylinders. This must have created something of a problem on the Spad, on which a stack-type exhaust (if one was in fact fitted) must have interfered with the pilot's view. Doubtless the Renault installation was an insurance against possible failure of the Hispano-Suiza. It was not developed.

The first two Spads VII to go to an operational unit are believed to have been S.112 and S.113, which were delivered to *Escadrille* N.3 on 2nd September, 1916. The first was allocated to Sergent Paul Sauvage, the second to Lieutenant Georges Guynemer. The 21-year-old Guynemer had until then flown the Morane-Saulnier parasol monoplane and Nieuport scouts with which his *escadrille* had been successively equipped and had at that time a victory score of some fourteen enemy aircraft.

It was almost as if the Spad had been designed with Guynemer in mind. He took to Béchereau's masterpiece immediately, and shot down a German aircraft on his second flight in the Spad. On 23rd September, 1916, three enemy aircraft fell to the Vickers gun of Guynemer's Spad. He was himself shot down in that combat but was unhurt. His victory total had risen to thirty by the end of January 1917. Delightedly, he called his Spad his *mitrailleuse volante* (flying machine-gun).

Escadrille N.3 was the first unit to be equipped throughout with Spads and was consequently re-designated SPA.3. It was one of the greatest of the French *escadrilles de chasse*, including in its members Capitaine Armand Pinsard (27 victories), Sous-Lieutenant René Dorme (23), Capitaine Alfred Heurtaux (21) and Capitaine Albert Deullin (20). Pinsard's first Spad in *Escadrille* SPA.3 was S.122.

By the end of October 1916 twenty-five Spads VII had been delivered to operational *escadrilles*. Despite the immense fighting value and relative scarcity of the new fighter, the French authorities generously made some Spads available to the R.F.C. within a few weeks of the emergence of the first production aircraft. Three were in British hands by the end of September 1916, and at least one of these was flying operationally before that month was out. This aircraft was with No. 60 Squadron, and on 28th September Captain E. L. Foot was flying it when he attacked four enemy aircraft and shot down one of them. On 20th September, 1916, Major General H. M. Trenchard, General Officer commanding the R.F.C., wrote to Colonel Barès asking for a further 30 Spads, and a week later Captain Lord Innes-Ker of the British Aviation Commission followed this up with a further letter suggesting that the 30 R.F.C. Spads might be built by Blériot Aéronautique. The French Minister of War gave his approval to this contract in a letter dated 5th October, 1916, on the understanding that the engines for the Spads would be supplied by the R.F.C. Among the earliest Spads used by the R.F.C. were those that had the British serial numbers A253, A256, A262, A263, A310 and A312. Of these, A256 is known to have been with No. 60 Squadron, R.F.C., on 10th October, 1916.

To both French and British authorities the Spad's quality was obvious, and both countries wanted more for their flying services. France's problem was that of expanding production: Britain's difficulty was how to obtain a share of the output of Spads. In France production was extended to a number of additional contractors, and eventually the Spad VII was built by the following companies in addition to the parent *Société anonyme pour l'Aviation et ses Dérivés*:

Blériot Aéronautique;
Les Ateliers d'Aviation L. Janoir;
Kellner et ses Fils;
Construction aéronautique Edmond de Marçay (built 1,800);

L'Atelier de construction d'Appareils d'Aviation Roger Sommer.
Les Ateliers de Construction Régy Frères (built 200);
Société d'Etudes Aéronautiques;
and the Grémont concern.

Corresponding arrangements for increasing production of the vital 150-h.p. Hispano-Suiza engine had to be made, and early deliveries of the Spad VII might have been larger if more engines had been available. Even with that engine the Spad did not long retain a sufficiently great advantage over the new German fighters that were introduced in the autumn of 1916. In December 1916 Guynemer told Béchereau:

"The 150-h.p. Spad is not a match for the Halberstadt. Although the Halberstadt is probably no faster it climbs better, consequently it has the overall advantage. More speed is needed: possibly the airscrew might be improved."

The Spad was given the fillip it needed by the development of the 180-h.p. Hispano-Suiza 8Ab engine. This was the 150-h.p. 8Aa engine with the compression ratio increased to 5.3:1; at full throttle it could produce 204 h.p. The 8Ab engine was fitted to French-built production aircraft as supplies became available. The first Spad VII to have the high-compression engine was allocated to Guynemer, who won 19 victories on the aircraft. During that strenuous period the engine was never changed, a remarkable record for the time.

Radiator shutters were fitted to the later Spads VII. On some aircraft these were disposed radially, but a simpler arrangement of vertical shutters was eventually standardized.

By 1st August, 1917, over fifty French *escadrilles de chasse* were equipped with the Spad, and there were 445 Spads VII with these units. A further 50 aircraft were with non-operational units; two of these had experimental installations of the 200-h.p. geared Hispano-Suiza 8B engine.

The supply of Spads to the Royal Flying Corps was a slow business. The first British unit to be selected for complete equipment with the Spad VII was No. 19 Squadron, R.F.C., which had earlier had the useless B.E.12. The first Spad to reach No. 19 Squadron was delivered in October 1916, but re-equipment was not complete until February 1917. In that month No. 23 Squadron received its first Spad but was not fully re-equipped until April 1917. A British contract for Spads was given to the Kellner firm in March 1917.

As both the R.F.C. and R.N.A.S. wanted Spads for their fighter squadrons arrangements were made for the

Said to be the Spad Type V, this aircraft certainly differed from the production Spad VII in having no exhaust pipes, an unusual arrangement of exhaust stubs, and no cover plates at the base of the fin over the single central elevator control lever. (Photo: Imperial War Museum Q.66749)

Early production Spad VII, without gun when photographed.   (Photo: Jean Noël).

Spad VII to be manufactured in England. Several specimen Spads VII were supplied to the British authorities: these included two acquired by the Admiralty and given the British serial numbers 9611 and 9612; S.211, another Admiralty purchase numbered N3399; and S.1321, which was given the British serial number A8965. The first Admiralty contract for Spads was for fifty aircraft (N6030 — N6079) ordered from the British Nieuport company in December 1916, but by February 1917 that batch of serial numbers was re-allocated for Nieuport-built S.E.5s for the R.N.A.S. This second allocation was short-lived, however: by 5th March the batch had again been changed to consist of Nieuport scouts. Further Admiralty contracts for one hundred Spads VII (N6210 — N6284 and N6580 — N6604) were given to Mann, Egerton & Co., Ltd., of Norwich; the latter group was subsequently reduced to N6580 — N6599. The War Office ordered 100 Spads from L. Blériot (Aeronautics) of Brooklands,* to be numbered A8794 — A8893.

* In February 1917 this company moved to Addlestone and changed its name to Blériot & Spad. Its further change of title to The Air Navigation Co., Ltd., did not occur until after Spad production had ceased at Addlestone.

The decision to deliver all British-built Spads to the R.F.C. and all Sopwith triplanes to the R.N.A.S. led to a change of identity for the Mann Egerton Spads. Apparently only N6210 was delivered wearing an N serial number. It was tested at Martlesham Heath and differed from the original French design in having a mounting for a Lewis gun above the upper wing. The ex-R.N.A.S. Spads were re-numbered A9100 — A9161 and B1351 — B1363; they were supplemented by B1364 — B1388 and B9911 — B9930, and it has been reported that the last twenty were those originally ordered as N6580 — N6599. The first Mann Egerton Spad, re-numbered A9100, was under test at Martlesham Heath in May 1917.

Blériot & Spad of Addlestone began deliveries in that month: A8794 and A8796 were at Farnborough on 19th May. The products of this firm left the factory with an enormous hooded fairing over the Vickers gun breech. Doubtless this was expected to make it easier for the

pilot to clear jams, and it was intended to serve as a windshield, but it obstructed forward view so seriously that it had to be removed. This modification must have retarded production. Other features of the British Blériot & Spad aircraft were unsatisfactory. Their radiators were regarded as inefficient, and a modification of the gun's magazine proved troublesome.

No doubt these changes in the original design were well-intentioned, for the original French-designed armament installation was not itself satisfactory. A burst of fire exceeding about twenty rounds imparted so much rotational momentum to the drum carrying the feed belt of ammunition that the belt could be forced on even after the gun ceased firing, causing a double feed. In No. 19 Squadron, R.F.C., this difficulty was overcome by replacing the drums by ammunition boxes.

Relatively few British-built Spads reached the squadrons in France. Their aircraft were mostly French-built, and as late as the summer of 1917 a further British contract for sixty 150-h.p. Spads was given to the firm of Kellner et ses Fils of Billancourt. It seems that the first two aircraft to be delivered under this contract were received by the R.F.C. in the first week of September 1917. Spads with the 180-h.p. 8Ab engine were also delivered to the R.F.C.; these aircraft were sometimes referred to as the Spad II.

The R.F.C. used the Spad in small numbers in the Middle East. Altogether nineteen were sent to that theatre of war, a few going to each of R.F.C. Squadrons Nos. 30, 63 and 72. These included the British-built Spads A8806 and A8812, which were used by No. 30 Squadron, and A8808, which went to No. 72 Squadron.

In 1917 Italy and Belgium received a small number of Spads VII. Fifteen delivered to Belgium were numbered Sp.1 to Sp.15 and equipped the 5e *Escadrille* (later re-numbered the 10e). It has been reported that the first of these was given to Edmond Thieffry and that he shot down an enemy aircraft the day after he received it.

Italy acquired more Spads than Belgium, the first in February 1917. These were widely used by the *squadriglie da caccia* side by side with Nieuports and Hanriots, among the Italian units known to have had some Spads VII being the 71a, 72a, 75a, 76a, 77a, 78a, and 91a *squadriglie.*

A brilliant Italian exponent of the Spad was Maggiore

One of the earliest production Spads VII arrives at an operational escadrille.

Francesco Baracca of the 91ª *squadriglia*. On 13th May, 1917, he shot down an Austrian Albatros D III as his first victory won on a Spad VII. His final victory score was 34 when he met his death in action on 19th June, 1918; about 23 of these were achieved on Spads VII and XIII.

Before the Russian revolution of October 1917, production of the Spad VII had begun at the Duks factory in Moscow. The type was subsequently flown by Russian pilots as part of the motley collection of aircraft, mostly of foreign origin, that had always composed the equipment of Russia's flying services.

The Spad VII was flown operationally on the Western Front by American pilots. Those serving with SPA.124, the *Escadrille Lafayette*, had become acquainted with the Spad when their unit was re-equipped in the spring of 1917. Nearly a year later, in February 1918, SPA.124 was transferred to the American Expeditionary Force as the 103rd Aero Squadron, U.S.A.S. At that time it still had a number of Spads VII for, as discussed below, early operational experience with the Spad XIII was by no means trouble-free, and the Spad VII had to soldier on much longer than has been generally believed.

From the French government the U.S.A.S. bought a total of 189 Spads VII; deliveries started in December 1917. As late as October 1918 some were allocated to the 138th and 638th Aero Squadrons, and later that year it was intended to equip the squadrons of the Fifth Pursuit Group with Spads VII.

In addition to the French-built Spads bought by the A.E.F., a number of British-built aircraft went to the U.S.A., where they remained in use for some years after the war. At least nineteen British Spads crossed the Atlantic. They were B1356 — B1361, B1372, B1374 — B1376, B1384, B1386, B9911, B9913, B9914, B9916, B9917, B9920 and B9924.

Production of the Spad VII in the U.S.A. was contemplated in 1917 shortly after America entered the war. A total of 3,000 aircraft was envisaged but the scheme was abandoned when it was realised that the Spad was not suitable for the Liberty aero-engine.

In addition to the two French Spads VII that had experimental installations of the 200-h.p. Hispano-Suiza, one or two abortive attempts were made in Britain to install 200-h.p. engines in Spads. A twin-gun variant with a 200-h.p. Hispano-Suiza under construction as the Blériot & Spad Addlestone works was reported to have been abandoned in July 1917 (possibly because the Spad XIII was then in prospect). A later British experiment was the installation of a 200-h.p. Wolseley Viper, reported to have been made in October 1917.

Native French developments with the 200-h.p. geared Hispano-Suiza had begun early in 1917. In January, at the request of Guynemer, work began on a development of the Spad VII in which a 37-mm *canon-Puteaux* was mounted between the cylinder blocks of a 200-h.p. geared Hispano-Suiza. This variant of the basic 200-h.p. Hispano-Suiza 8B was designated 8C. The shell-firing gun was installed with its breech in the cockpit, its barrel passing through the hollow airscrew shaft. Additionally, a single Vickers gun was mounted on top of the fuselage to starboard, lying in a trough in the top cowling. The resulting aircraft was designated Spad XIICa.1, in appearance very similar to the Spad VII but in reality a different aircraft. Its loaded weight of 800 kg (1,958 lb.) was 185 kg (407 lb.) greater than that of the Spad VII; its wing area was 20.2 sq. m. (217.4 sq. ft.), whereas that of the earlier type had been 18 sq. m. (193.7 sq. ft.).

On the Spad XII the mainplanes had quite a large radius of curvature at the leading edge and were rigged with slight positive stagger. Advantage was taken of the higher thrust line of the geared engine to fit a cowling that required no protuberant fairings over the camshaft housings; and an enlarged rudder with a curved trailing-edge contour was fitted.

Guynemer was flying his Spad XII by early July 1917. He called it his *avion magique*, and won his 49th, 50th, 51st and 52nd victories on it. The Spad XII was put into production, and 300 were built. René Fonck flew the Spad XII S.445 for part of his wartime career and won no fewer than eleven victories on it.

But for less skilled pilots the Spad XII was rather too much of a handful. The 37-mm gun was a single-shot weapon and had to be re-loaded by hand during combat, thus demanding exceptionally accurate flying and marksmanship. Vibration was one of the several troubles that plagued the geared Hispano-Suiza, and this affected marksmanship adversely. The heavy recoil and fumes in the cockpit made the Spad XIICa.1 unpopular.

Nevertheless, it was officially regarded as a standard type. Later production aircraft had the 220-h.p. Hispano-Suiza 8Cb which increased the Spad XII's maximum speed from 197 km/hr (123 m.p.h.) to 212 km/hr (132.5 m.p.h.). As late as July 1918 one Spad XII was sold to the U.S.A. and was allocated to the 13th Aero Squadron, then at Belrain, where it was flown by the commanding officer, Major C. J. Biddle, in early October 1918. Biddle has recorded that this Spad XII was to have been flown by Lt. D. E. Putnam of the 139th Aero Squadron, but Putnam was killed on 14th September, 1918, consequently the aircraft went to Biddle.

Contemporary with the Spad XIICa.1 in the S.P.A.D. drawing office was the Spad XIIIC.1. This was a wholly separate design intended to exploit the standard 200-h.p. Hispano-Suiza 8B engine and more conventional armament of twin Vickers guns mounted above the engine. The prototype Spad XIII is believed to have been S.392, which was flown by Sous-Lieutenant René Dorme at Buc on 4th April, 1917.

This first Spad XIII was demonstrated to French fighter squadrons by Maurice Prévost, and the first production aircraft emerged towards the end of May 1917. The initial contract was for 250 Spads XIII but production was slow to gather momentum. By 1st August only seventeen had been delivered and six more were at the experimental establishment at Villacoublay.

Large-scale production was planned. As early as April 1917, before the prototype could have been fully evaluated, it was estimated that 2,230 Spads XIII would be delivered by 31st March, 1918. This optimistic forecast was made before the persistent troubles that bedevilled the 200-h.p. Hispano-Suiza had manifested themselves: in fact, only 764 Spads XIII had been completed by 31st March, 1918, and of that total only 290 were in operational service on 1st April.

The Spad XIII was generally similar to the Type VII, having the same characteristic interplane bracing with mid-bay H-shaped king-post members. The engine cowling reverted to having projecting fairings over the camshaft housings, but the frontal radiator opening had a sharp edge without camber, and radiator shutters were a standard fitting.

On the first production version of the Spad XIII the mainplanes were quite different from those of the Spads VII and XII, for they had well-rounded tips and the ailerons had inverse taper with slightly curved trailing edges. The centre-section struts had forward stagger, and a bracing wire connected the top of the forward strut to the upper longeron on each side.

As they became available Spads XIII were issued to the *escadrilles de chasse*, either as replacements for Spads VII or as new equipment. Fortunately, production of the Spad VII did not cease: indeed, during the first quarter of 1918 a total of 1,220 Spads VII were built compared with some 630 Spads XIII.

Guynemer had a Spad XIII shortly before his death and must have won his final victories while flying it. His was a standard early production aircraft with rounded wing tips and the early centre-section bracing. *Le grand chasseur* disappeared on 11th September, 1917, not quite 23 years old and with a victory score of 54. Although fourteen months of bitter fighting were to elapse before the war ended, only René Fonck was to surpass Guynemer in the final list of French aces. Fonck, too, was a brilliant exponent of the Spad XIII.

In October 1917, in a letter to the French Ministry of War, Général Pétain stated bluntly that the Nieuport scouts then in service were inferior to all contemporary enemy fighters and that it was essential that, by the spring of 1918, French fighter squadrons should be equipped exclusively with Spads or the Nieuport 28. With the abandonment of the Nieuport 28 the need for enormous numbers of Spads became vital.

It became equally essential to improve the reliability of the 200-h.p. Hispano-Suiza engine. In a report submitted in early 1918 Général Pétain recorded that mechanical faults had rendered unserviceable two-thirds of the Spads XIII with operational units. By the end of February 1918 the Under-Secretary of State was informed that there was an almost total lack of spares for Hispano-Suiza engines.

Spad XIII, French Naval Air Service, Dunkirk 1918.

Fortunately, the production of engines with better-quality reduction gears, coupled with independent remedial work by Marc Birkigt on the engine's lubrication, improved the situation. By March 1918 the parent S.P.A.D. company was producing Spads XIII at the rate of eleven per day, and the type was built by eight other contractors, namely:

A.C.M. (built 361);
Adolphe Bernard (1,750);
Blériot Aéronautique (2,300);
Société anonyme des Etablissements Borel (300);
Kellner et ses Fils (1,280);
Pierre Levasseur (340);
Société des Etablissements Nieuport (700);
Société anonyme française de Constructions Aéronautiques (300).

With the 1,141 Spads XIII built by the parent company, total production thus reached 8,472 by the time it ceased in 1919.

The great majority of the production aircraft were of a modified type in which the wing tips reverted to a blunt, squarish shape rather similar to that of the Spad VII. In these later aircraft the centre-section bracing was strengthened by fitting a substantial faired tie-rod on each side between the top of the forward centre-section strut and the upper longeron, thus forming what looked like an inverted-V strut supporting the forward spar of the upper wing.

Additionally, the 200-h.p. Hispano-Suiza 8B was superseded by the 220-h.p. 8Be, a high-compression version of the basic geared engine, and the cowling round the radiator was again given slight camber. Later still, the 235-h.p. Hispano-Suiza 8BEc improved the Spad XIII's performance further.

The modified Spads XIII were available early in 1918. By that time No. 23 Squadron, R.F.C., had been re-equipped with Spads XIII, and it seems that their first blunt-wing aircraft was B6882, which was known in the squadron as the "clipped-wing experimental Spad".

Spads XIII were also supplied to Italy and Belgium. The 91ᵃ *squadriglia* of the *Aeronautica del Regio Esercito* was re-equipped with Spads XIII in October 1917. As noted above, this was Francesco Baracca's unit, and he flew the Spad XIII until his death.

Belgian use of the Spad XIII began in March 1918, when the new type began to replace the Spads VII of the 10ᵉ *escadrille*. The Spad XIII remained in squadron service in Belgium for several years after the war.

But second only to France in terms of numbers of aircraft used was the U.S. Air Service, which bought a total of 893 Spads XIII. Deliveries of these started in March 1918, and it seems that all had the modified wings and either the 220-h.p. Hispano-Suiza 8Be or the 235-h.p. 8BEc engine. The aircraft were issued to the 13th, 17th, 22nd, 27th, 28th, 49th, 93rd, 94th, 95th, 103rd, 139th, 141st, 147th, 185th and 213th Aero Squadrons during 1918. In all, 328 Spads XIII were in U.S.A.S. service in France on 11th November, 1918.

The Spad was well-liked by the American squadrons, and was flown with considerable success by such pilots as Rickenbacker and Luke. It featured in the vastly ambitious aircraft manufacturing programme that was just getting under way in the U.S.A. when the Armistice was signed. At that time three contracts for 6,000 American-built Spads XIII were cancelled. Had these American Spads been completed they would most probably have been armed with two Marlin machine-guns in place of the standard pair of Vickers. A few Spads in American service were in fact armed with Marlins.

An interesting member of the Béchereau-desgined family of Spad fighters was the Spad XIV of 1917. This was a single-seat fighter seaplane with a twin-float undercarriage. It had the fuselage, Hispano-Suiza 8C engine and 37-mm shell-gun armament of the Spad XII with, of course, the single Vickers machine-gun; but in every other respect the Spad XIV was a completely different aircraft. Its wing span was 9.8 m. compared with the 8.0 m. of the Spad XII and the 8.08 m. of the Spad XIII; the wing area of the Spad XIV was 26.2 sq. m.

The mainplanes were braced as a wholly conventional two-bay structure with cross-bracing in each bay, and the forward centre-section support on each side was an inverted-V strut. Although of typical Béchereau-Spad appearance, the tail surfaces were larger than those of the Spad XII. The undercarriage consisted of two Tellier-built main floats only: there was no tail float. These were relatively broad in the beam, but had steps and were of quite good form.

The prototype Spad XIV was built by Pierre Levasseur and made its first flight on 15th November, 1917. It was demonstrated brilliantly by Béquet, and on test proved to have a maximum speed of 205 km/hr (128 m.p.h.), which was claimed to be a record for seaplanes at that time. Forty production aircraft were ordered for the fighter units of the *Aviation maritime*, and it seems that some may have been used operationally at Dunkerque and Corfu.

Late in 1918 a landplane version of the Spad XIV was built. The designation Spad XXIV has been attributed to this type, which may have been intended as a ship-board fighter comparable with the Sopwith 2F.1 Camel. The Spad XXIV (if such it was) did not fly until 5th November, 1918, consequently it was not developed.

The Spad XV was the first Spad type designed by Herbemont and, with its monocoque fuselage, was completely different in conception from the Béchereau designs. The Spad XVI was a slightly modified Spad XI, and the next Béchereau design was the Spad XVII. This was the ultimate development of the basic Béchereau configuration.

It embodied the final wartime version of the Hispano-Suiza, the 300-h.p. 8F, a direct-drive engine that completed its bench tests in February 1918. One had been fitted to a specially strengthened Spad by mid-April 1918.

In general, the Spad XVII looked like a bulkier version of the Spad XIII; its overall dimensions were identical with those of the earlier type. The radiator of the Spad XVII was appreciably larger, the rear fuselage was more carefully faired with multiple stringers, and the rudder profile was again altered. The loaded weight went up to 944 kg (2,077 lb.) but, despite the more powerful engine, the aircraft's performance was virtually identical with that of the final form of the Spad XIII with the 235-h.p. Hispano-Suiza 8BEc engine. The Spad XVII's operational trials were flown by Capitaine de Slade in June 1918 and twenty examples of the type were built before the war ended. It has been reported that some of these were allocated to leading pilots of the *Groupe de Combat les Cigognes*.

With the departure of Louis Béchereau from the S.P.A.D. to join the S.A.B. design bureau, responsibility for design lay with Herbemont, who produced his advanced Type XVIII/XX/XXI fighters. The last vestige of Béchereau's influence was to be seen in the curious Spad XXII. This consisted of a slightly modified Spad XVII fuselage fitted with completely re-designed wings of which the upper was somewhat similar to that of Herbemont's Spad XX. On the XXII, however, the tip shape had the blunt contour favoured by Béchereau and the ailerons were on the upper wings (on the Herbemont types they were on the lower wings). The upper wing of the Spad XXII had three spars and pronounced sweep-back; the lower had appreciable sweep-forward and, as on the Spad XVII, was braced to the undercarriage by cables. The tailplane was braced by a V-strut, and the elevators were horn-balanced.

The Spad XXII was powered by the 300-h.p. Hispano-Suiza engine. Its extraordinary wing configuration was adopted in a radical endeavour to improve the pilot's field of view, but it is doubtful whether any improvement that it might have achieved would have justified the manufacturing and maintenance problems that it must have created. Perhaps fortunately, the end of the war frustrated any development of the Spad XXII.

© J. M. Bruce, 1969.

Above: S.1647 in the markings of Escadrille SPA 3. (Photo: Imperial War Museum Q.64215)

Below: Spad VII with the wild boar insignia of Escadrille SPA 57. (Photo: Musée Royal de l'Armée et d'Histoire Militaire, Brussels).

Below: Believed to be of Esc. SPA 102, this Spad VII had a personal emblem on the aft fuselage in addition to the Escadrille marking. (Photo: E. C. Armées).

Left: Spad VII of unknown unit. (Photo: E. C. Armées).

Above: Spad VII S.7139 in camouflage paint scheme. (Photo: Jean Noël).

Below: Spad VII wearing the handsome insignia of SPA 31. This aircraft had the generous windscreen fitted to many French-built Spads. (Photo: Musée Royal de l'Armée et d'Histoire Militaire, Brussels).

Above: Another Spad VII of SPA 31. This one was captured intact on 6th April 1917 by Jasta 38.   (Photo: Peter M. Bowers).

Below: S.1461 of SPA 93 had a star, presumably red, painted above the upper starboard wing.   (Photo: Musée Royal de l'Armée et d'Histoire Militaire, Brussels).

Four aspects of a liberally marked Spad VII in German hands. This aircraft had an unusual arrangement of radiator shutters.
(Photos via Peter M. Grosz)

Above: Possibly of SPA 12, this Spad VII had full-depth vertical radiator shutters. The nose of the engine cowling was painted a light colour. (Photo: Musée Royal de l'Armée et d'Histoire Militaire, Brussels).

Below: Detail view of the aircraft in the preceding illustration. (Photo: Musée Royal de l'Armée et d'Histoire Militaire, Brussels).

Above: This crashed Spad VII displays one of the standard French camouflage schemes and the elegant shape of its tailplane and elevators.

Right: On this damaged Spad VII the close-set main spars of the upper wing and the close pitch of its full-chord ribs can be seen. (Photo: Jean Noël).

Below: Spad VII with rocket-launching rails on the mid-bay struts. Note metal sheathing of lower wing. (Photo: Imperial War Museum Q.67932).

Right: Starboard side of Spad VII nose, in this instance with wire-netting panel in place of louvred cowling panel for maximum cooling. The actuating shaft of the Birkigt synchronizing mechanism can be seen running up to the rear of the Vickers barrel casing. (Photo: Musée de l'Air).

Left: Nose detail of Spad VII with cowling panel removed.

Right: Cockpit of Spad VII. (Photo: Musée Royal de l'Armée et d'Histoire Militaire, Brussels).

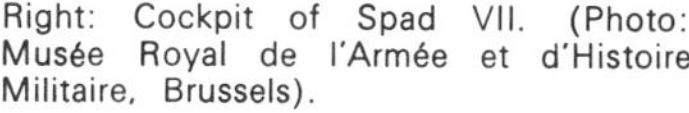

Left: The primitive method of stowing the ammunition belt on the Spad VII. The forward drum held the loaded belt; the empty belt was wound on to the rear drum. (Photo: Museé de l'Air MA 1422).

Below: View over the gun of a Royal Flying Corps Spad VII. Note how on British Spads the wing fabric was stitched to every rib, with a frayed-edge fairing strip doped on over the stitching.

Left: Spad VII fitted with camera gun. (Photo: Peter M. Bowers).

Above: Spad VII S.211 with the British serial number N3399, all numerals in both identifying numbers being applied in the same style of characters. (Photo: Peter M. Bowers).

Above: S.1321 was supplied to the War Office as A8965. (Photo: Imperial War Museum Q55998).

Above: The first Spad VII built by Mann, Egerton & Co., Ltd., at Martlesham Heath, wearing its original serial number N6210. (Photo: Royal Aeronautical Society).

Below: Rear view of N6210 shows small cut-away in trailing edge of upper wing for Lewis gun mounting. (Photo: Royal Aeronautical Society).

Above: Mann, Egerton Spad VII, probably N6210. This aircraft had a modified radiator cowling with re-entrant leading edge that must have reduced the efficiency of the radiator.   (Photo: Imperial War Museum Q.67971).

Above: Renumbered A9100, the first Mann, Egerton Spad VII is here seen with its Lewis gun in position.   (Photo: Royal Aeronautical Society).

Below: The second Spad built by Mann, Egerton & Co., Ltd., was marked in a different style. It was apparently used by a training squadron or unit.   (Photo: Flight International 19335).

Above: A8794, the first Spad built at Addlestone by Blériot & Spad. It is here seen at Farnborough, with the clumsy hooded windshield in front of the cockpit.   (Photo: Imperial War Museum MH3506).

Above & below: These two photographs of A8801 illustrate more clearly the large opaque windshield fitted to the earliest Spads VII built by Blériot & Spad at Addlestone.   (Photos: Imperial War Museum Q55997 and Q56000).

Above: A8804 modified in the same way as A8798 and re-marked in service with its serial number in unusually large characters.

Below: Lieutenant Balme of No. 23 Squadron R.F.C., beside his Spad VII B3460 shot down on 10th October 1917 by Gefreiter Brettel of Jagdstaffel 10. The markings on the radiator cowling are noteworthy; they appeared on other Spads of No. 23 Squadron.   (Photo: Egon Krueger).

Below: A6706, one of the French-built Spads VII flown by No. 19 Squadron, R.F.C., wearing the black dumb-bell marking used by that unit in the spring of 1917.   (Photo: Ministry of Defence H.1179)

Above: A French-built Spad VII with No. 17 Squadron, R.F.C., in Macedonia. The pilot, Major J. H. Herring, was the Officer Commanding No. 17 Squadron at the time, and is now (in 1969) Group Captain J. H. Herring, D.S.O., M.C., R.A.F. (ret'd). It is believed that this and the following photograph were taken on Mikra Bay aerodrome near Salonika.   (Photo: P. R. Little).

Below: This close-up of Major Herring's Spad shows that its shortened exhaust pipes were cut away.

Fifth aircraft of the batch of Spads VII built by Blériot & Spad, A8798 is here seen after the removal of the clumsy windshield. (Photo: Ministry of Defence H.1019).

Right: This photograph is of unusual interest, for it depicts Spads VII of the 103rd Aero Squadron, U.S.A.S., after that unit (the former Escadrille Lafayette) transferred to the U.S.A.S. in February 1918, and shows that the 103rd was still flying Spads VII at that time. (Photo: Peter M. Bowers).

Right: French-built Spad VII at McCook Field for experimental purposes. (Photo: Peter M. Bowers).

Below: Among the British-built Spads VII that went to the U.S.A. was B1357, here seen at Rockwell Field. (Photo: Warren M. Bodie).

Left: Also photographed in the U.S.A. was this Mann, Egerton Spad B9913. It is believed that this is the Spad that was rebuilt by Jim Petty and now, wearing spurious markings, is in the Canadian National Aviation Museum. (Photo: Peter M. Bowers).

Right: The first Spad to enter Belgian service bore the Belgian identity Sp.1 on the rudder. It is here seen at Les Moëres. (Photo: Jean Noël).

Above: The Belgian Spad VII Sp. 2 was the aircraft of Second Lieutenant C. Ciselet and is here seen in the colourful markings of the 5e Escadrille (Escadrille Comète).   (Photo: Musée Royal de l'Armée et d'Histoire Militaire)
Below, two pictures: Second Lieutenant C. Ciselet with his Spad Sp.2.   (Photos: Musée Royal de l'Armée et d'Histoire Militaire).

Below: Belgian Spad VII of the 5e Escadrille, note red nose.   (Photo: Musée Royal de l'Armée et d'Histoire Militaire).

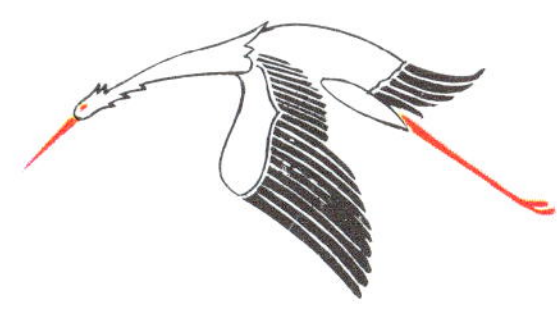

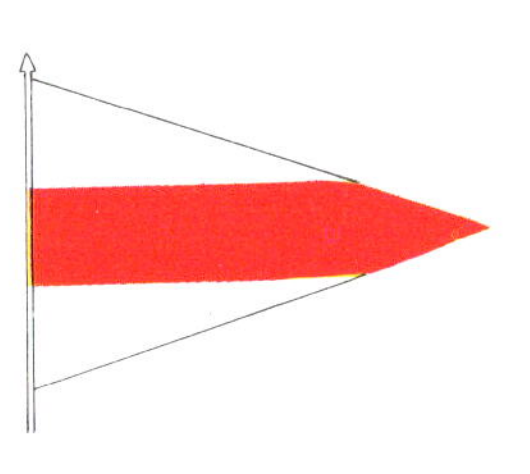

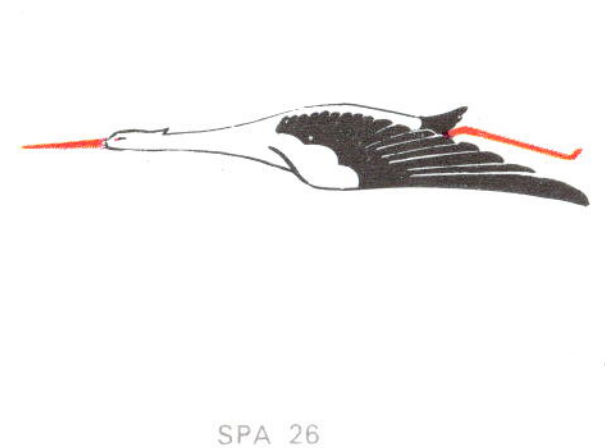

1 SPAD VII, Escadrille SPA 3 flown by Capitaine Georges Guynemer. S 245.

2 SPAD VII, Escadrille SPA 3. S 1647.

3 SPAD XIII, Escadrille SPA 3, flown by Capitaine Georges Guynemer, 1917.

4 SPAD XIII, Escadrille SPA 48, flown by Capitaine Armand de Turenne. Serial unknown.

5 SPAD VII, Escadrille SPA 37. S 1389.

ESCADRILLE SPAD INSIGNIA

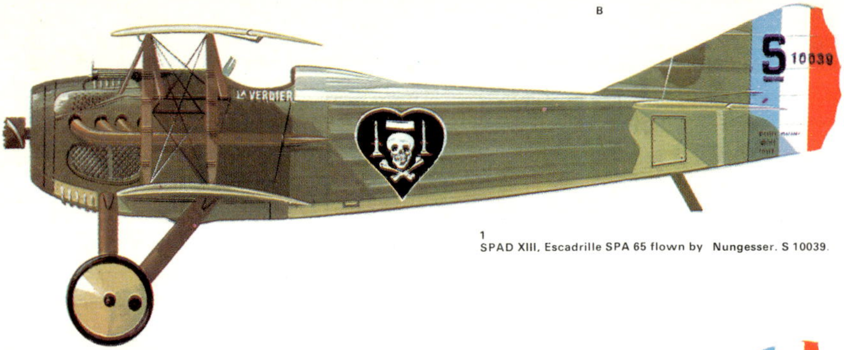

1
SPAD XIII, Escadrille SPA 65 flown by Nungesser. S 10039.

2
SPAD VII, Escadrille SPA 77. S 5152.

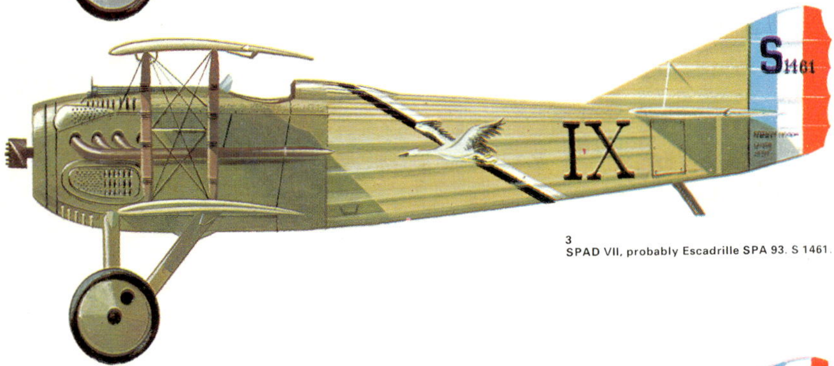

3
SPAD VII, probably Escadrille SPA 93. S 1461.

4
SPAD VII, Escadrille SPA 99. S 3281.

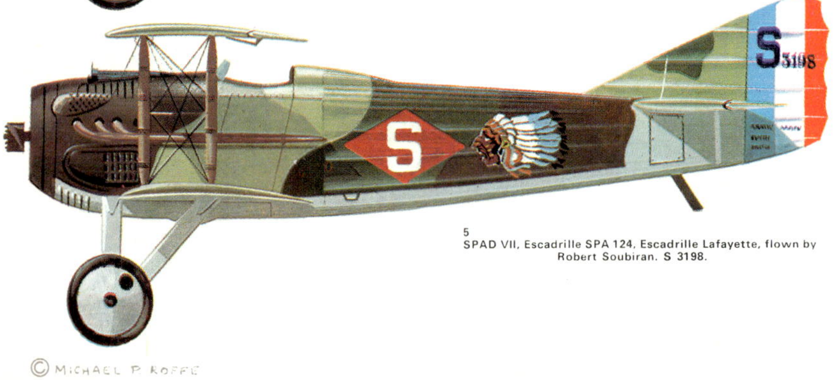

5
SPAD VII, Escadrille SPA 124, Escadrille Lafayette, flown by
Robert Soubiran. S 3198.

© MICHAEL P. ROFFE

1
SPAD XIII, Escadrille SPA 151. S 654.

2
SPAD XIII, Escadrille SPA 159. S 497.

3
SPAD VII, flown by Adjutant Maxine Lenoir, killed in action 25th October 1916; 11 victories. S 116.

4
SPAD VII, 10th Escadrille, Aviation Militaire Belge. Sp.1.

5
SPAD VII, 10th Escadrille, Aviation Militaire Belge. Sp.2.

© WARD

© MICHAEL P. ROFFE

1
SPAD XIII, Aviation Militaire Belge, Sp. 30.

2
SPAD VII, the first SPAD VII to be built by Mann, Egerton & Co. Ltd., N6210.

3
SPAD VII, N 6210 renumbered on transfer to the Royal Flying Corps, A 9100.

4
SPAD VII, unit unknown, Royal Flying Corps. S 211/N3399.

5
SPAD VII, No. 19 Squadron, Royal Flying Corps. December 1917. A6662.

© MICHAEL ROFFE

ESCADRILLE SPAD INSIGNIA

SPA 68

SPA 69

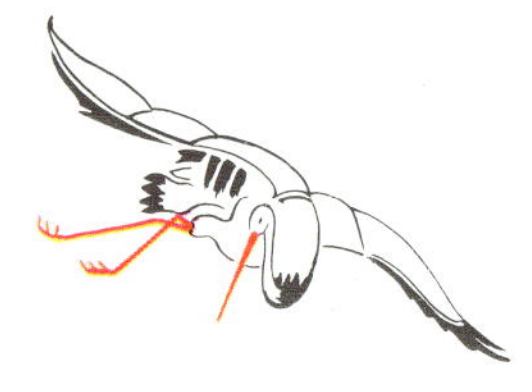

SPA 73

SPA 75

SPA 76

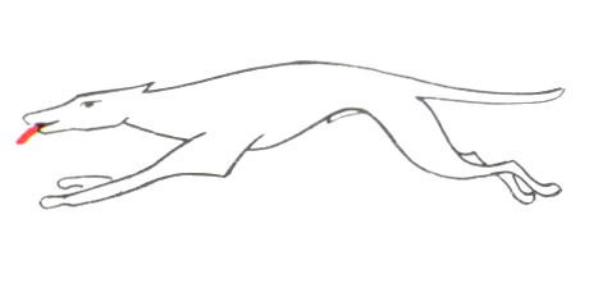

ESCADRILLE SPAD INSIGNIA

1
SPAD VII, No. 19 Squadron, Royal Flying Corps, April 1917. A 310.

2
SPAD VII, No. 19 Squadron, Royal Flying Corps, A 6706.

3
SPAD VII, No. 19 Squadron, Royal Flying Corps, May 1917. B 1537.

4
SPAD VII, No. 19 Squadron, Royal Flying Corps. B1627.

5
SPAD VII, No. 19 Squadron, Royal Flying Corps, flown by Lt. A. R. Boeree. B3520.

© MICHAEL P. ROFFE

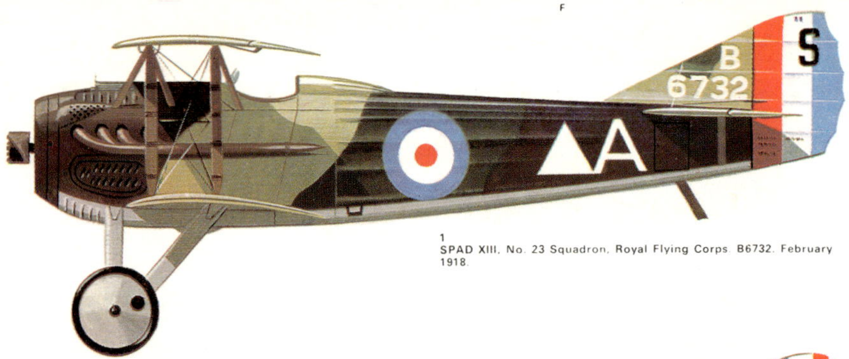

1
SPAD XIII, No. 23 Squadron, Royal Flying Corps. B6732. February 1918.

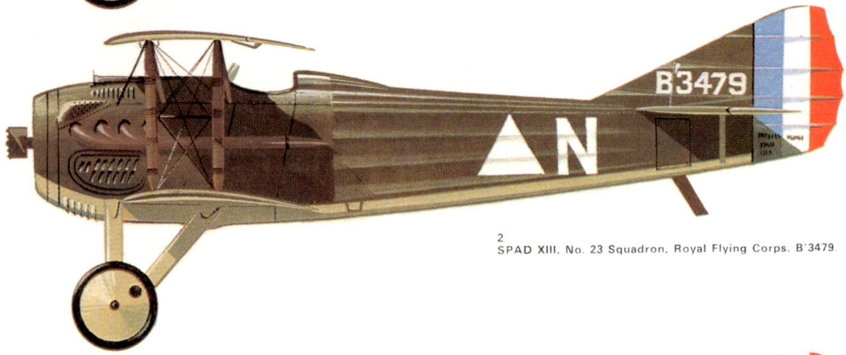

2
SPAD XIII, No. 23 Squadron, Royal Flying Corps. B3479. 1918.

3
SPAD VII, unit unknown, Royal Flying Corps. S 1321 A8965.

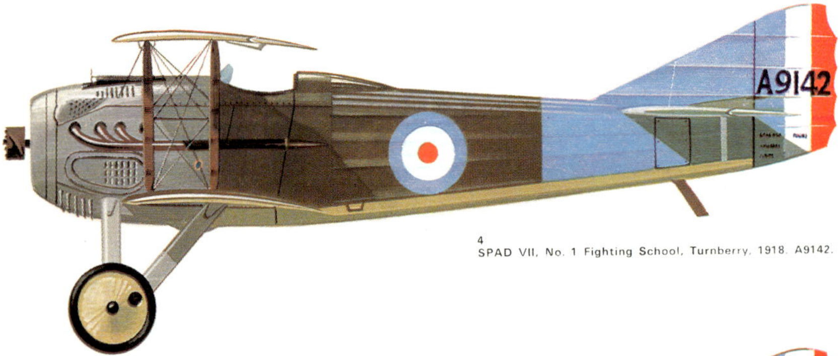

4
SPAD VII, No. 1 Fighting School, Turnberry, 1918. A9142.

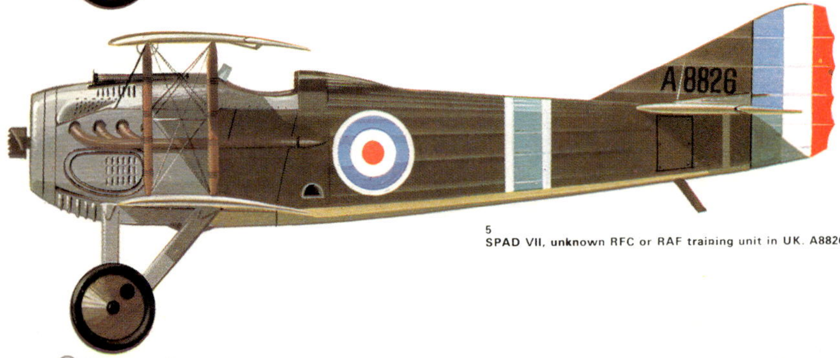

5
SPAD VII, unknown RFC or RAF training unit in UK. A8826.

© MICHAEL P. ROFFE

ESCADRILLE SPAD INSIGNIA

SPA 83

SPA 84

SPA 85

SPA 86

SPA 87.

© WARD

ESCADRILLE SPAD INSIGNIA

SPA 89

SPA 90

SPA 91

SPA 92

SPA 93

G

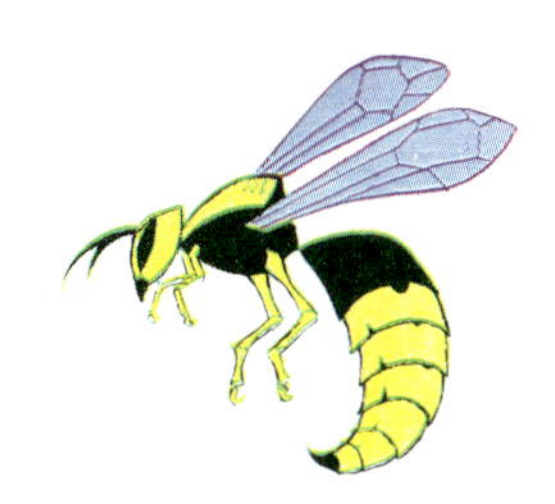

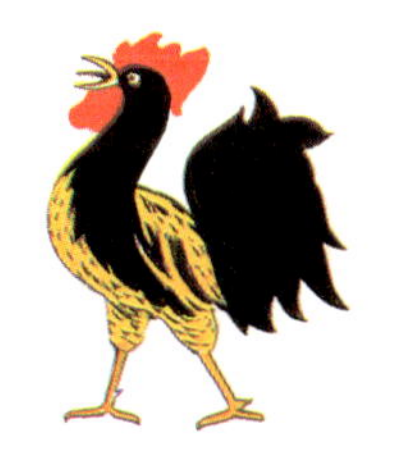

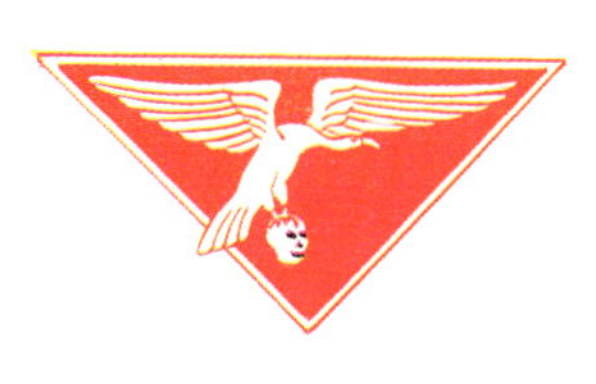

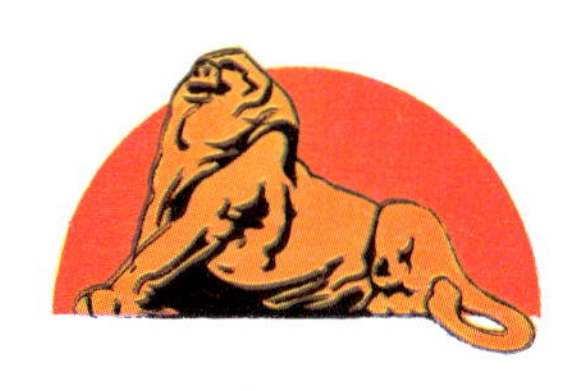

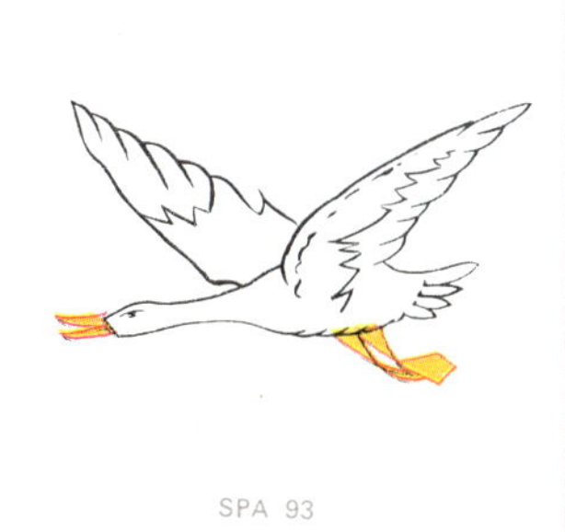

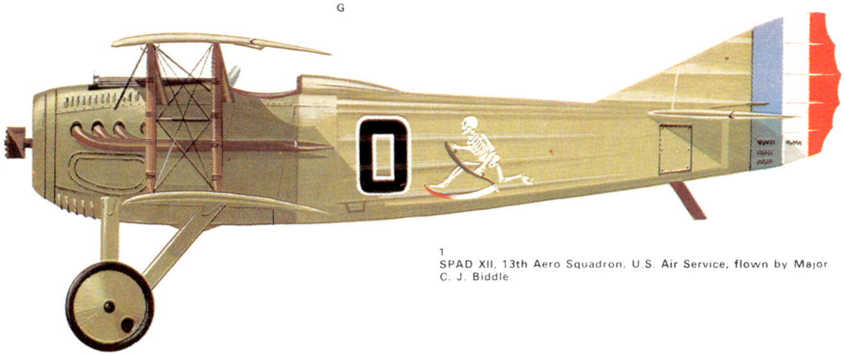

1
SPAD XII, 13th Aero Squadron, U.S. Air Service, flown by Major C. J. Biddle

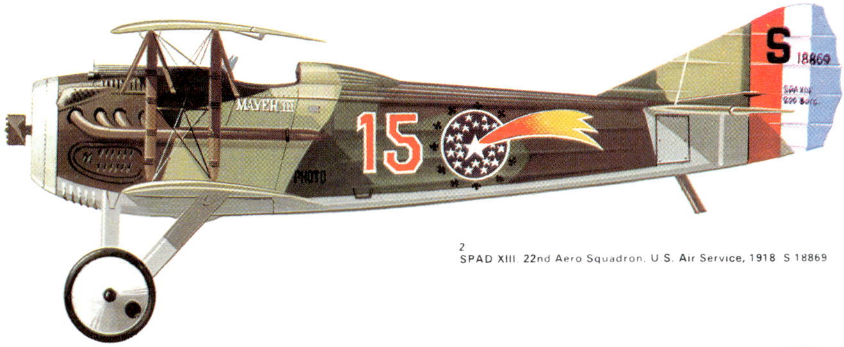

2
SPAD XIII. 22nd Aero Squadron, U.S. Air Service, 1918 S 18869

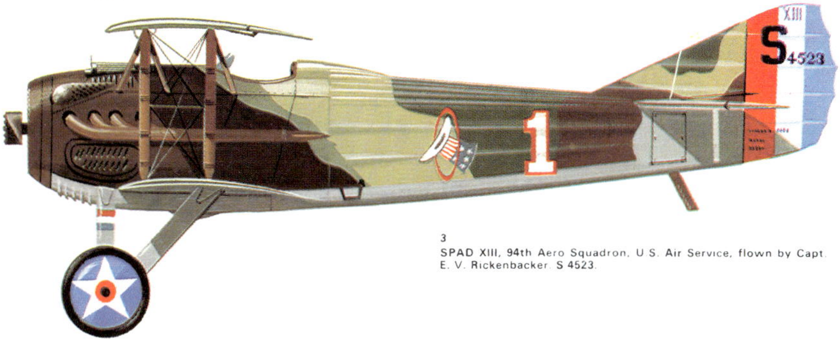

3
SPAD XIII, 94th Aero Squadron, U.S. Air Service, flown by Capt. E. V. Rickenbacker. S 4523.

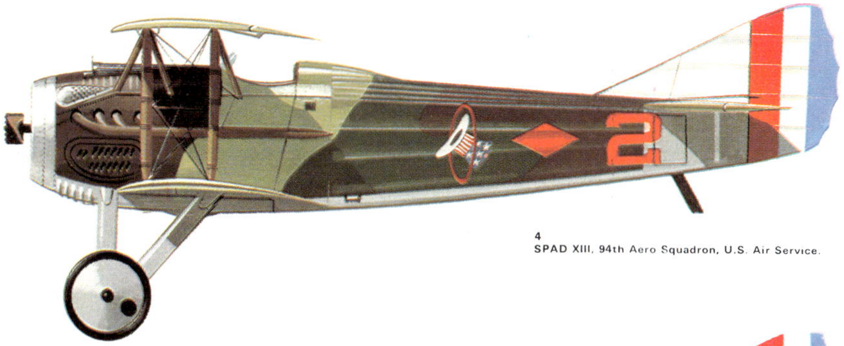

4
SPAD XIII, 94th Aero Squadron, U.S. Air Service.

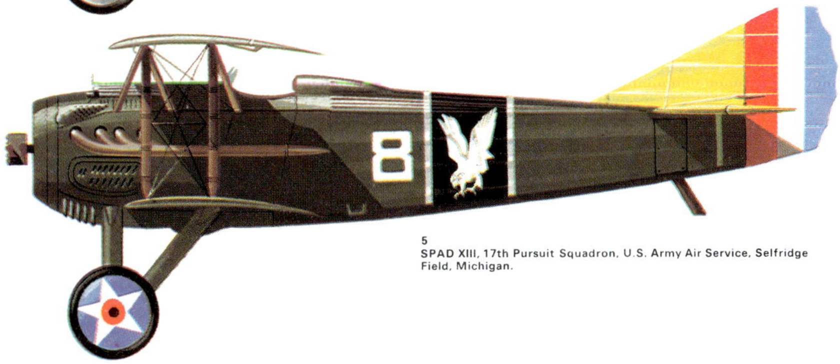

5
SPAD XIII, 17th Pursuit Squadron, U.S. Army Air Service, Selfridge Field, Michigan.

H

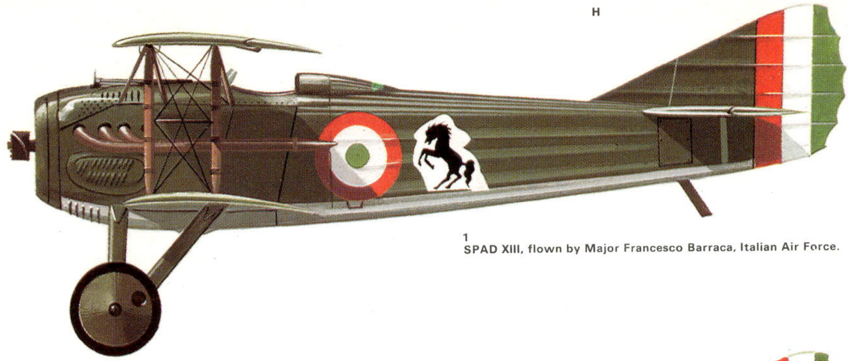

1
SPAD XIII, flown by Major Francesco Barraca, Italian Air Force.

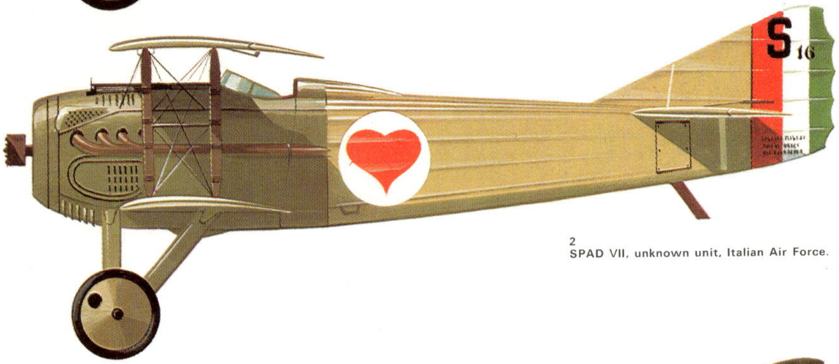

2
SPAD VII, unknown unit, Italian Air Force.

3
SPAD XIII, Polish Air Force.

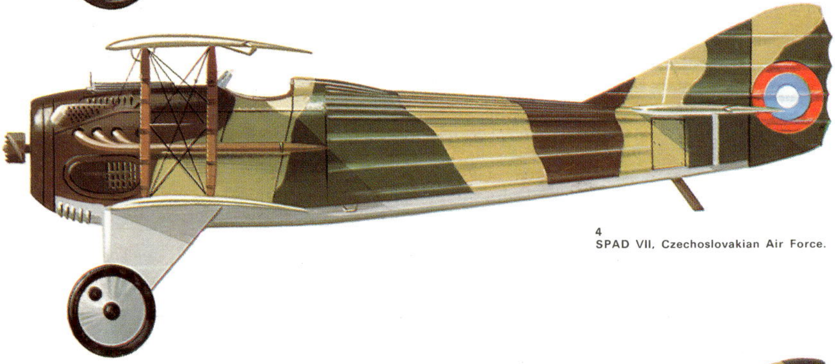

4
SPAD VII, Czechoslovakian Air Force.

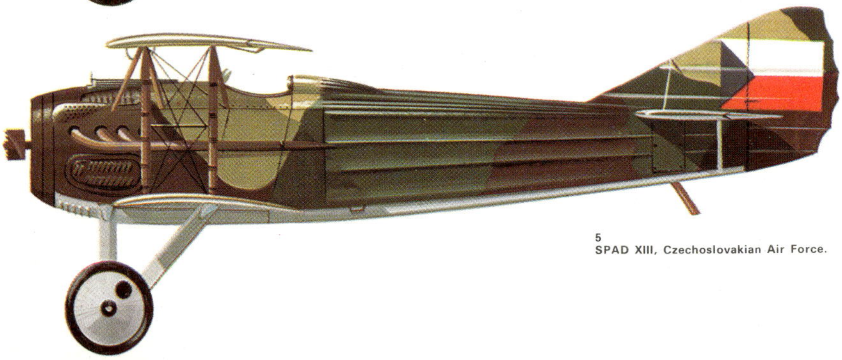

5
SPAD XIII, Czechoslovakian Air Force.

© MICHAEL P. ROFFE

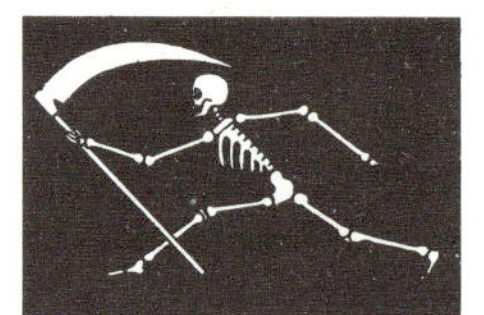

© WARD

Above: Thieffry beside his Spad. Note the slightly different rendering of the 5e Escadrille marking from that of Ciselet's aircraft.   (Photo: Musée Royal de l'Armée et d'Histoire Militaire).

Above: Second Lieutenant Edmond Thieffry (10 victories) of the Belgian 5e Escadrille with his Spad VII.   (Photo: Musée Royal de l'Armée et d'Histoire Militaire).

Below: Czechoslovakian Spad VII with faired undercarriage legs.   (Photo: Zdeněk Titz).

Above: A Spad VII in Italian service.   (Photo: Imperial War Museum Q.67931).

Left: A Spad VII in U.S. Air Service markings after the Armistice. Note that the stars were painted with a point lying aft.   (Photo: Peter M. Bowers).

Below: A Spad VII of the U.S. Marine Corps at Rockwell Field. The markings cannot be confirmed as an official scheme. (Photo: Warren M. Bodie).

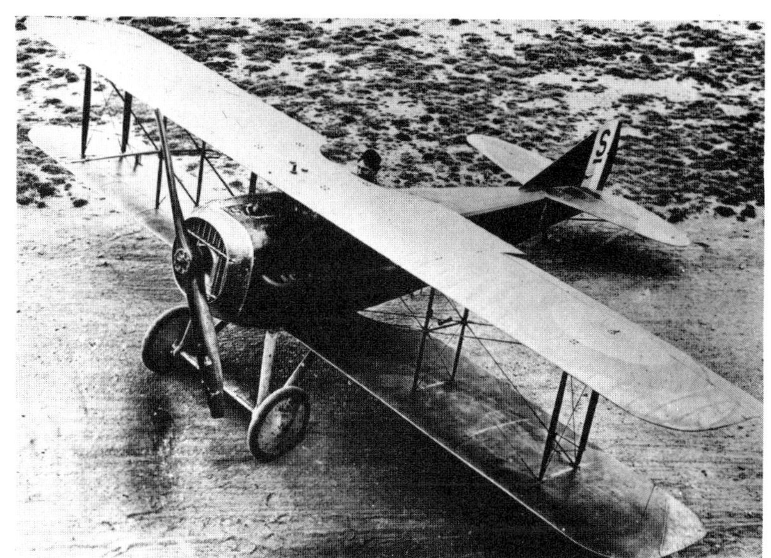

Right: This photograph of the Spad XII S.440 shows the characteristic shape of the radiator cowling and the trough for the single Vickers gun. (Photo: Imperial War Museum Q.46118).

Below: Another view of the Spad XII S.440. (Photo: Imperial War Museum Q.58417).

Below: Major Charles J. Biddle, Officer Commanding the 13th Aero Squadron, U.S. Air Service, in the only Spad XII to be allocated to the U.S.A.S. It was marked with the Grim Reaper insignia of the 13th Aero Squadron, and the individual numeral 0 identified it as the squadron commander's aircraft.

Above: This front view of an early production Spad XIII illustrates clearly the fully rounded wing tips of the aircraft of the initial production series.

Above: Guynemer's Spad XIII, an early-production aircraft with round wing tips and the original arrangement of centre-section struts. It is believed that this photograph was taken at St. Pol. In the background, at left, is a Sopwith triplane.

Below: The Belgian aerodrome at Les Moëres, 10th September 1917. Georges Guynemer works on the troublesome engine that obliged him to land there in his Spad XIII. On the following day he disappeared. (Photo: Musée Royal de l'Armée et d'Histoire Militaire).

Capitaine Armand de Turenne (15 victories) with an early Spad XIII of Escadrille SPA 48.   (Photo: Jean Noël).

These four views of an early Spad XIII, S.497 of Escadrille SPA 159, illustrates the wing-tip planform, original centre-section bracing and radiator cowling of this version of the type.   (Photos: Peter M. Grosz).

Spads XIII of Escadrille SPA 151.   (Photo: Jean Noël).

Above and below: Spad XIII No. 4523 flown by Captain E. V. Rickenbacker, 94th Aero Squadron, U.S. Air Service. (Photos: U.S. Signal Corps).

The Spad XIII flown by Captain E. V. Rickenbacker (26 victories) of the 94th Aero Squadron. U.S. Air Service. (Photo: Peter M. Bowers).

One of the Spads XIII that went to the U.S.A. after the Armistice, here seen at Selfridge Field, Michigan, in the markings of the 17th Pursuit Squadron, U.S. Army Air Service. (Photo: Fred C. Dickey Jr.).

A Spad XIII in Belgian service.

Below: Typical Spad XIII of the revised production type with blunt wing tips, strengthened centre-section bracing and modified radiator cowling This aircraft was of the 94th Aero Squadron, U.S. Air Service.   (Photo: Royal Aeronautical Society).

Below: After the Armistice, many American Spads XIII were given colourful individual markings. This one, photographed in 1919, was of the 94th Aero Squadron.   (Photo: Peter M. Bowers).

Above: Among the heterogeneous collection of aircraft flown by the Czechoslovak Army Air Force soon after its formation were some Spads. A Spad XIII in early Czechoslovak markings is seen here.

Below: Substantial numbers of French and British aircraft were supplied to Poland in 1919, among them several Spads VII and XIII. This photograph depicts a Spad XIII in Polish markings.   (Photo: J. B. Cynk).

Above: This photograph of a Spad XIV shows that it was anything but a mere floatplane version of the Spad XII. It had wings of greater span with fully-braced two-bay bracing and enlarged tail surfaces.   (Photo: Musée de l'Air).

Above: Although the landplane version of the Spad XIV is recorded, apparently authoritatively, as the Spad XXIV, this aircraft bore in tiny letters on its rudder the marking S.XIV. (The designation Spad IX is wholly erroneous.)   (Photo: Musée de l'Air).

Below: One of the small number of Spads XVII that were built, S.733. (Photo: Musée de l'Air).

The Spad XXII had a remarkable wing arrangement with heavy sweepback on the upper mainplane and equally pronounced sweep-forward on the lower.   (Photo: Imperial War Museum Q.66756).

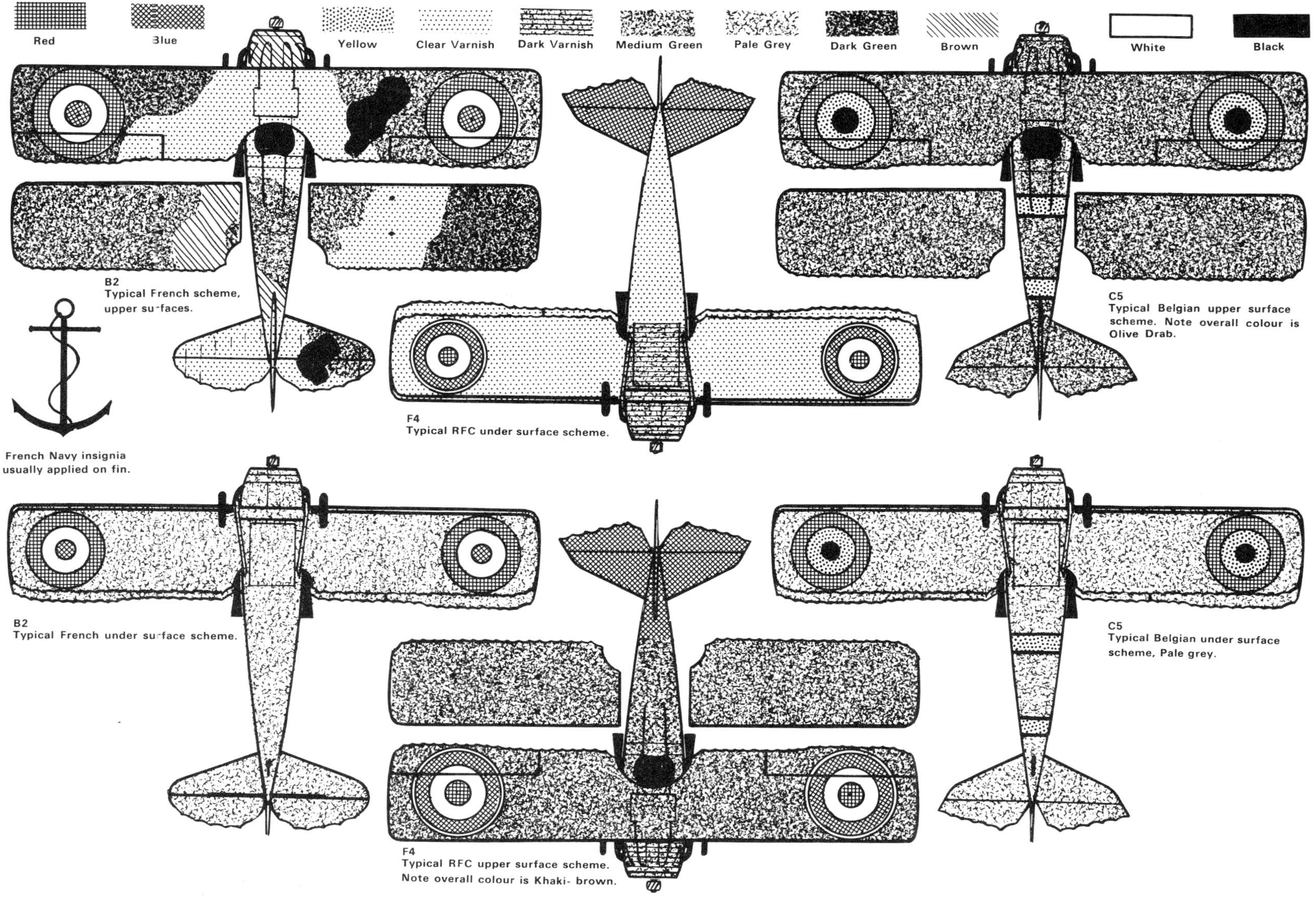

Red
Blue
Yellow
Clear Varnish
Dark Varnish
Medium Green
Pale Grey
Dark Green
Brown
White
Black
B2
Typical French scheme, upper su-faces.
French Navy insignia usually applied on fin.
F4
Typical RFC under surface scheme.
C5
Typical Belgian upper surface scheme. Note overall colour is Olive Drab.
B2
Typical French under surface scheme.
F4
Typical RFC upper surface scheme. Note overall colour is Khaki- brown.
C5
Typical Belgian under surface scheme, Pale grey.

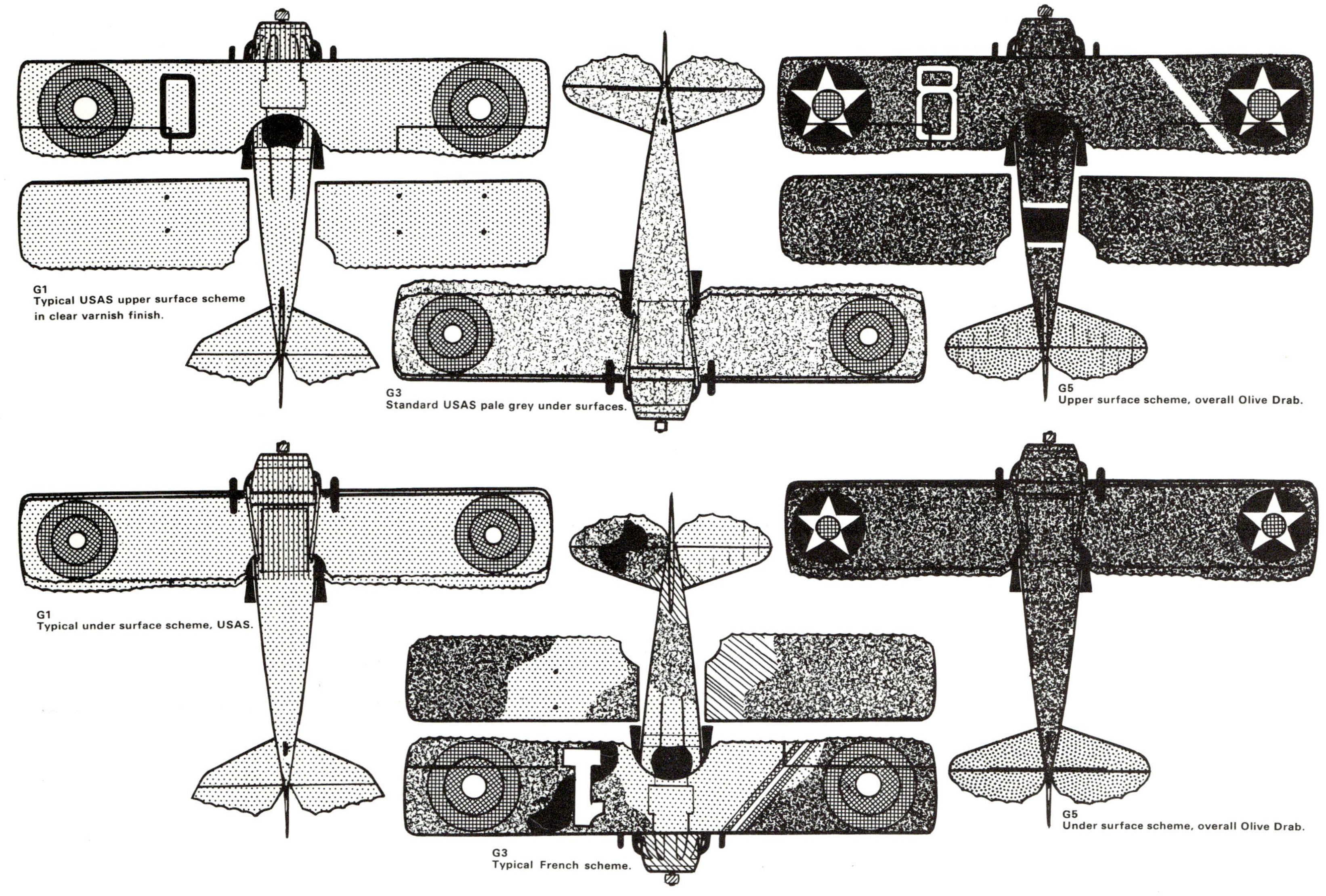

G1
Typical USAS upper surface scheme in clear varnish finish.
G3
Standard USAS pale grey under surfaces.
G5
Upper surface scheme, overall Olive Drab.
G1
Typical under surface scheme, USAS.
G3
Typical French scheme.
G5
Under surface scheme, overall Olive Drab.